-Cooking's Cool -
Seasonal Family Favorites
- Mrs. Sheff's Top 50 Recipes for Your Family Table -

Cooking.
Magical.
Fun.

Recipes by: Cindy Sardo, author of the *Cooking's Cool* Book Series
Illustrations by: Penny Weber
Graphic Design by: Carla Genther

Also by Cindy Sardo:
Cooking's Cool in the Fall
Cooking's Cool in the Winter
Cooking's Cool in the Spring
Cooking's Cool in the Summer

- Mrs. Sheff's -
Tips for the Chefs

Safety is key to enjoying a great cooking experience.
Follow these simple tips during your journey of becoming a great chef!

1. Wash hands and pop on a chef's hat before beginning to cook.
2. Always have adult supervision when cooking.
3. Use safe cutting tools like pizza cutters or scissors. Always have adults use the knives.
4. Make sure you wash the vegetables or fruit before you use them.
5. Use potholders to handle hot pots or cookie sheets.
6. Wear an apron while you cook in the kitchen.
7. Clean up as you go while you are cooking.
8. Get all ingredients cleaned, chopped or measured before you begin to cook.
   This is known as "mise en place" which means put in place.
9. Watch your fingers if you are using graters or peelers to grate your own cheese or peel your vegetables.
10. Cook together frequently as a family.

- Mrs. Sheff's -
Fall Recipes

Mini Apple Pies

Mini fruit pies are just plain adorable. These mini apples pies are topped with a delicious streusel topping that your kids will adore! Perfect for individual pies for your guests at your next Thanksgiving table.

Prep time: 30 minutes   **Total time:** 1 hr. 15 min.

Yields 6 servings

5 apples, *peeled & sliced*
1 Tbsp. white whole wheat flour
1 lemon, *juiced*
2 tsp. cinnamon
½ cup sugar
Dash of salt
1 box store-bought pie crust
12 mini pie pans

Streusel Topping:
¾ cup flour
¼ cup granulated sugar
¼ cup light brown sugar
¼ tsp. kosher salt
1 cup rolled oats
1 stick cold unsalted butter, *diced*

Directions:

1. Preheat oven to 375°.

2. Peel and slice the apples and place in a large bowl.

3. Squeeze lemon over the apples. Add flour, sugar and dash of salt.

4. Add cinnamon and stir to combine.

5. Prepare streusel topping by combining flour, salt and oats.

6. Add butter to mixture. Cut in small pieces.

7. Cut the pie crust into 6 circles that are 6 inches in diameter. Place in 5 inch mini pie pans.

8. Add apple mixture to each mini-pie pan and top with streusel topping.

9. Bake until brown and bubbly. *Approximate time: 30-40 minutes.*

Draw how a pumpkin grows in a pumpkin patch.

"Go apple picking with your family." ~ Mrs. Sheff

Pumpkin Waffles

What says fall more than pumpkins? These little pumpkin waffles make weekend breakfasts in the fall a delight. Top with a crunch of mixed nuts and pumpkin seeds and the sweetness of pure maple syrup.

Prep time: 15 minutes   **Total time:** 1 hour

Yields 8 servings

½ cup oats
½ cup whole wheat flour
1 Tbsp. ground flaxseed
2 tsp. baking powder
¼ tsp. pumpkin pie spice
¼ tsp. salt
1 egg, *separated*
¾ cup low fat milk

¼ cup banana, *mashed*
1 Tbsp. canola oil
Toppings:
  A blend of nuts
  Dried cranberries
  Pumpkin seeds
  Maple syrup

Directions:

1. Process oats in a food processor. Combine with remaining dry ingredients.
2. Whisk egg whites until peaks form.
3. Combine milk, banana, oil and egg yolk. Gently stir.
4. Fold in egg whites.
5. Cook in a waffle iron. *Approximate time: 5 minutes*.
6. Top waffles with the blend of nuts, dried cranberries, pumpkin seeds and maple syrup.

D1308523

Cookwork

Why is quinoa so healthy? What are some other super healthy foods?

_____

_____

_____

_____

_____

_____

_____

_____

_____

"Fill your refrigerator with a variety of fruits and vegetables." ~ Mrs. Sheff

Crazy Quinoa Salad

Quinoa is an easy way to pack protein into a salad. The delicate texture of the quinoa combines well with a dice of crisp, raw veggies and crumbled feta cheese in this salad. And a lemon infused vinaigrette makes this salad irresistible.

Prep time: 15 minutes   **Total time:** 90 minutes

Yields 8 servings

1 cup quinoa
¾ cup olive oil
¼ cup golden basalmic vinegar
Juice of 1 lemon
Salt & pepper
1 cucumber, *diced*

1 green bell pepper, *diced*
1 small can of black olives, *sliced*
½ cup spinach cut into thin strips
1 container grape tomatoes, *quartered*
½ cup feta cheese, *crumbled*

Directions:

1. Cook quinoa according to package directions.

2. Run quinoa under running cold water.

3. Prepare dressing by combining olive oil, vinegar, lemon juice and seasonings in a mason jar. Shake.

4. Combine diced cucumber, pepper, tomatoes, spinach and cheese with the quinoa.

5. Add dressing. Stir.

6. Refrigerate the salad for at least 1 hour before serving.

Cooking.
Magical.
Fun.

Cookwork

Search for other recipes for Shepherd's Pies.

_____

_____

_____

_____

_____

_____

_____

_____

"Bring the farm to your table in your home." ~ Mrs. Sheff

Mini Shepherd's Pies

Ever try a shepherd's pie made with chicken? This twist on the classic recipe is made with chicken and combined with a traditional mix of vegetables. Mashed potatoes top off this yummy, comforting dish.

Prep time: 15 minutes   **Total time:** 1 hour

Yields 6-8 servings

4 potatoes, *peeled and diced*
2 Tbsp. olive oil
1 small onion, *finely chopped*
3 carrots, *diced*
3 celery stalks, *diced*
2 Tbsp. parsley, *chopped*

1 ~ 32 oz. container of chicken broth
1 cooked chicken breast, *shredded*
2 Tbsp. flour
½ cup low fat milk, *warmed*
½ cup parmesan cheese
2 oz. cream cheese

Directions:

1. Bring half box of stock to a boil and add chicken. Let simmer until cooked thoroughly. *Approximate time: 20 minutes.* Shred.

2. Meanwhile bring 4 cups salted water to a boil. Add diced potatoes and cook until fork tender. *Approximate time: 12 minutes.*

3. Over medium heat, add 1 tablespoon olive oil to a large skillet. Add onion, carrots and celery. Season with salt and pepper. Sauté until soft. *Approximate time: 5 minutes.*

4. Add flour to skillet and sauté for a minute. Add remaining chicken broth into skillet and stir.

5. Reduce heat to low. Add shredded chicken, peas and chopped parsley. Stir.

6. Drain potatoes and mash with a potato masher. Add warm milk and cheeses.

7. Preheat your broiler.

8. Spoon chicken and veggies into mini-pie tins. Top each pie with mashed potatoes.

9. Broil until golden brown.

Design your own colorful vegetable garden.

Add a fancy gate and label the vegetables planted in your garden.

"Plant a garden in your backyard!" ~ *Mrs. Sheff*

Harvest Salad Jars

Time to celebrate the autumn with a variety of fall favorites layered into a mason jar. Crisp apples, pecans, pumpkin and pomegranate seeds give flavor and great nutrition to salad served not on a plate but rather in a fun, little mason jar!

Prep time: 15 minutes   **Total time:** 1 hour

Yields 4 servings

2 cups fresh spinach, *thinly sliced*
1 head Romaine lettuce, *thinly sliced*
1 can black beans, *drained and rinsed*
1 cup pecans or pieces
1 pint yellow grape tomatoes, *quartered*
2 honeycrisp apples, *diced*
½ cup pumpkin seeds or toasted pepitas

¼ cup pomegranate seeds
Dressing:
 ¼ cup golden balsamic vinegar
 ¾ cup olive oil
 Juice of a lemon
 Salt & Pepper

Directions:

1. Layer all of the ingredients into a mason jar in a colorful pattern.

2. Combine all of the ingredients to make the dressing into a mason jar or bowl and shake or whisk to combine.

3. Add the apple in at the end to prevent browning.

4. Pour dressing into each jar.

5. Top additionally if desired with feta cheese, chopped egg or chopped bacon.

Cookwork

Search for some other toppings that you could put on your pops. What other bread or muffin recipes could you make into a pop?

_____

_____

_____

_____

_____

_____

_____

_____

"Happiness is knowing where your food is grown." ~ Mrs. Sheff

Banana Bread Pops

These pop in your mouth bites of banana bread are simply scrumptious! Kids will adore their taste and have tons of fun making these healthier than most treats.

Prep time: 15 minutes **Total time:** 45 minutes

Yields 6 servings

3 ripe bananas
1 cup applesauce
2 eggs
1 tsp. baking soda
1 Tbsp. baking powder
½ tsp. salt
1 tsp. vanilla extract

2 cups whole wheat white flour
Glaze:
 3 Tbsp. butter
 1 cup confectioners sugar
 1 tsp. vanilla
 Roll in colorful sugars

Directions:

1. Preheat oven to 350°.

2. Place bananas in a large bowl and mash with an electric mixer.

3. Add applesauce and the eggs and beat well.

4. Next add in the baking soda, baking powder, salt and vanilla.

5. Then gradually add in the flour to this mixture until well combined.

6. Add 1 small ice cream scoop of the batter to a cake pop machine or small muffin pan.

7. Let cook for 5 minutes in cake pop machine or bake for 10 minutes at 350° in the oven.

Cookwork

What is traditionally in ratatouille? Where does the word originate?

_____

_____

_____

_____

_____

_____

_____

_____

"Set a pretty family dinner table." ~ Mrs. Sheff

Ratatouille Pasta

This pasta recipe is a twist on a classic French recipe ~ ratatouille. Tomatoes, onions, garlic and zucchini are paired with a rotini pasta. What could be better? Top with a sprinkle of parmesan cheese.

Prep time: 15 minutes   **Total time:** 30 minutes

Yields 4-6 servings

2 Tbsp. olive oil
4 tomatoes, *seeded and diced*
2 zucchini, *diced*
1 small onion, *finely chopped*

2 cloves garlic, *finely chopped*
½ cup parmesan cheese
1 lb. whole grain pasta
Salt & pepper

Directions:

1. Cook pasta according to package directions. Reserve ½ cup pasta water.

2. Over medium heat, add olive oil to a sauté pan.

3. Add garlic and sauté until soft and fragrant. *Approximate time: 3 minutes.*

4. Then add the tomato and zucchini and sauté for 10 minutes.

5. Combine pasta, vegetables and reserved cooking liquid.

6. Sprinkle with parmesan cheese and salt & pepper to taste.

Cooking. *Magical.* Fun.

Search for Roasted Vegetable Quesadillas.

```
V  I  N  D  V  V  D  E  T  S  A  O  R  P  U
T  M  E  L  T  E  D  G  W  M  R  W  C  U  Z
G  S  R  Q  Z  B  K  K  C  A  J  X  T  J  L
M  O  N  T  E  R  E  Y  U  Z  U  E  W  G  I
M  Z  F  R  M  O  Y  S  O  H  R  C  Z  X  O
B  A  K  E  S  A  L  L  I  D  A  S  E  U  Q
S  P  A  X  B  K  I  G  C  O  P  E  F  Y  B
R  O  X  F  L  V  C  F  P  M  B  B  W  F  W
E  N  D  R  E  V  S  T  O  R  R  A  C  Y  X
P  I  A  L  L  I  T  R  O  T  O  A  H  P  F
P  O  F  E  H  G  K  X  Y  O  Z  C  V  R  R
E  N  I  N  I  H  C  C  U  Z  B  R  I  W  V
P  U  J  C  H  E  E  S  E  E  R  E  X  O  F
U  Q  E  L  B  A  T  E  G  E  V  D  A  X  W
L  L  Z  R  O  V  V  W  V  H  M  W  Q  Y  R
```

Bake	Jack	Oil
Onion	Red	Vegetable
Carrots	Melted	Olive
Peppers	Roasted	Zucchini
Cheese	Monterey	
Quesadillas	Tortilla	

Roasted Vegetable Quesadillas

Everybody loves a quesadilla especially those filled with roasted vegetables. This will be a family favorite so make extra for school lunches the next day.

Prep time: 15 minutes   **Total time:** 45 minutes

Yields 4 servings

1 green pepper, *thinly sliced*
1 red pepper, *thinly sliced*
1 zucchini, *thinly sliced*
1 small red onion, *thinly sliced*
2-3 Tbsp. olive oil

2 cups pepper jack or cheddar cheese *shredded*
8 whole grain or whole wheat tortillas
Salt & pepper

Directions:

1. Preheat oven to 400°.
2. Slice all of the vegetables into thin strips and place on a cookie sheet.
3. Sprinkle vegetables with olive oil and season with salt and pepper.
4. Roast vegetables for 20-25 minutes.
5. Arrange vegetables and cheese between 2 flour tortillas.
6. Grill on a griddle or in a sauté pan over medium heat. *Approximate time: 4-5 minutes per side.*

Cooking.
Magical.
Fun.

Brainstorm **a list of different types of soup.**

_____

_____

_____

_____

_____

_____

_____

_____

_____

"Take turns picking the meals for the week" ~ *Mrs. Sheff*

Cauliflower Soup

This delicious soup is perfect to enjoy on a cold, winter evening. A sauté of carrots, onion and celery not only bring color to the soup but also adds distinctive flavor. Top soup with crispy breadcrumbs and serve with a salad.

Prep time: 10 minutes   **Total time:** 30 minutes

Yields 6-8 servings

1 head of cauliflower, *cut*
2 carrots
1 small onion
2 stalks of celery
1 32 oz. box of chicken stock

1 ½ cups low-fat milk
Salt & pepper
Toppings:
   Cheddar cheese

Directions:

1. Over medium heat, sauté carrots, onion and celery in pan until soft and fragrant. Set aside. *Approximate time: 5 minutes.*

2. Bring chicken broth to a boil. Add cut cauliflower.

3. Reduce heat to medium and let cauliflower simmer in broth until tender. *Approximate time: 20-30 minutes.*

4. Purée the soup with an immersion blender or a regular blender. Place a towel over the top to prevent a spill.

5. Reduce heat to low and add milk. Season with salt and pepper.

6. Add sautéed vegetables and stir to combine until heated thoroughly.

Crispy Breadcrumbs

Over medium heat add 2 tablespoons of olive oil to a skillet. Add 1/2 cup panko breadcrumbs and let toast until golden brown ~ 5 minutes. Add 1 tablespoon chopped parsley and season with salt and pepper.

Draw your Tiny Tacos.

"Be inspired by the passion of other chefs." ~ *Mrs. Sheff*

Tiny Tacos

Baked tortilla chips filled with a homemade salsa! These tiny tacos are perfect for parties or an after-school snack.

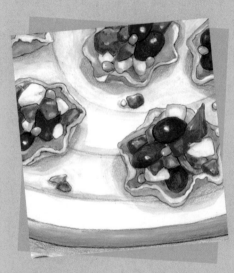

Prep time: 15 minutes   **Total time:** 30 minutes

Yields 4-6 servings

1 small onion, *finely chopped*
½ can black beans, *drained & rinsed*
1 cup fresh or frozen corn thawed
1 tomato, *diced*
3 Tbsp. olive oil

2 Tbsp. red wine vinegar
1 cup fresh mozzarella
 boccocini, *quartered*
Corn scoop style tortillas chips, *baked*

Directions:

1. Combine all of the ingredients in a large bowl.
2. Cover and let marinate in the refrigerator for an hour.
3. Spoon mixture into the tiny tortilla chips.

Cooking.
Magical.
Fun.

Create your own fall recipe.

Ingredients

Prep time: ___minutes   **Total time:** ___minutes

Yields ____ servings

_____

_____

_____

_____

_____

_____

_____

_____

"Let the magic begin in your family kitchen." ~ Mrs. Sheff

Veggie Chili

Everybody loves chili on a crisp fall day. This variation is made will all vegetables. The mix of colors and textures will make this a family favorite for you next party or Sunday dinner!

Prep time: 15 minutes   **Total time:** 45 minutes

Yields 4 servings

2 Tbsp. olive oil or canola oil	2 tsp. cumin
1 medium red onion, chopped	2 tsp. chili powder
1 green pepper, chopped	Salt & Pepper
1 orange pepper, chopped	Cheddar or Monterey Jack cheese
1 poblano chili pepper, chopped	Tortilla chips
1 small can corn	*Toppings:*
1 cup reduced sodium black beans	Cilantro
1 ~ 28 oz. can crushed tomatoes	Sour Cream

Directions:

1. Over medium heat, sauté onion and garlic in oil.
2. Add chopped peppers and sauté until soft. *Approximate time: 5 minutes.*
3. Season with cumin, chili powder and salt and pepper.
4. Add 1 can of crushed tomatoes.
5. Add in 1 can of corn and 1 cup black beans.
6. Let simmer for 30 minutes.

Cooking.
Magical.
Fun.

Create a hearty breakfast recipe.

Ingredients

Prep time:___minutes   **Total time:**___minutes

Yields ____ servings

"Start your day off with a healthy breakfast." ~ *Mrs. Sheff*

Pumpkin French Toast

Savor the taste of pumpkin with this twist on classic French toast. This yummy breakfast will delight children during the fall season. Serve with warm maple syrup and sliced fruit.

Prep time: 10 minutes   **Total time:** 30 minutes

Yields 6-8 servings

2 eggs	⅛ tsp. salt
½ cup low-fat milk	1 Tbsp. butter
¼ cup pumpkin	6-8 slices whole grain white,
½ tsp. vanilla	wheat or cinnamon bread
½ tsp. cinnamon	

Directions:

1. Beat eggs and gradually add in milk.
2. Stir in pumpkin, vanilla and cinnamon.
3. Over medium heat, melt 1 tablespoon butter in a skillet or griddle.
4. Dip bread slices into egg mixture.
5. Sauté bread on each side until golden brown.

- Mrs. Sheff's -
Winter Recipes

Butternut Squash
Mac & Cheese

What kid does not love macaroni and cheese? This is a twist on this kid classic with a sweet and savory mix. The sweetness of the roasted butternut squash and the saltiness of the cheddar cheese will make this a favorite in your home.

Prep time: 15 minutes   **Total time:** 1 hour

Yields 8 servings

1 lb. vegetable pasta
3 Tbsp. flour
3 Tbsp. butter
2 cups low-fat milk
8 oz. low-fat cheddar cheese, *grated*

2 Tbsp. olive oil
1 butternut squash,
 peeled and diced
1 cup spinach, *thinly sliced*
Salt & pepper

Directions:
1. Preheat oven to 425°.
2. Peel and dice the butternut squash and place on a cookie sheet.
3. Drizzle with olive oil and season with salt and pepper.
4. Roast butternut squash for 20-30 minutes until tender or carmelized.
5. Chop spinach in thin strips. Set aside.
6. Cook pasta according to package directions.
7. Melt butter over low heat in saucepan.
8. Add flour and whisk to combine for about 1 minute over low heat.
9. Over medium heat, add milk and let sauce thicken. Whisk occasionally. *Approximate time: 2 min.*
10. Add grated cheddar cheese. Stir to combine.
11. Add roasted butternut squash and spinach. Stir to combine.

Cookwork

Search for other recipes for Monkey Bread.

_____

_____

_____

_____

_____

_____

_____

_____

"You will love the Mini Monkey Breads as a special treat!" ~ Mrs. Sheff

Mini Monkey Bread

Monkey Bread is a fun breakfast recipe that is enjoyed by children and adults alike. Make them mini and you have an even more adorable treat! Kids love to cut and roll the biscuits using a pizza cutter and cutting board. Serve them with a colorful fruit salad for a weekend breakfast or brunch.

Prep time: 25 minutes   **Total time:** 1 hour

Yields 8 servings

1 ~ 8 count canister of biscuits
¼ cup brown sugar
¼ granulated sugar
1 Tbsp. cinnamon
2 Tbsp. butter, *melted*

1 tsp. vanilla
Toppings:
  Nuts
  Cranberries
  Pumpkin Seeds

Directions:
1. Preheat oven to 350° and spray large muffin pan with canola cooking spray.
2. Combine sugars, cinnamon, butter and vanilla.
3. Cut each biscuit into eights, like a pizza, with a pizza cutter.
4. Roll each triangle into a ball. Roll in sugar mixture.
5. Place all 8 balls in one section of the muffin pan.
6. Sprinkle with toppings.
7. Bake for 20-25 minutes.

Draw your bowl of polenta.

"Color a rainbow for your refrigerator to remind your family to eat a rainbow each day" ~ Mrs. Sheff

Roasted Vegetable Polenta

Roasted vegetables make polenta scrumptious. The nutty flavor of the vegetables when roasted pairs well with the creaminess of the polenta. Roast the vegetables in advance for a quick weeknight meal. This dish is colorful and delicious!

Prep time: 20 minutes　　**Total time:** 50 minutes

Yields 6-8 servings

2 Tbsp. olive oil
1 zucchini, *diced*
2 tomatoes, *diced*
½ red onion, *diced*
1 cup baby carrots, *diced*
1 yellow pepper, *diced*
1 clove garlic, *grated*

2 cups instant polenta
2 ½ cups chicken stock
½ cup low-fat cheese, *shredded* Cheddar/Monterey mixture
2 Tbsp. agave
2 Tbsp. butter
Top with fresh basil, *chopped*

Directions:

1. Preheat oven to 425°.
2. Dice all vegetables and place on a cookie sheet.
3. Drizzle with olive oil and season with salt and pepper.
4. Roast vegetables in oven. *Approximate time: 20-25 minutes.*
5. In large saucepan, bring water & chicken stock to rapid boil. Whisk in polenta and stir until creamy and thick. *Approximate time: 3 minutes.*
6. Turn off heat and stir in cheese, agave, and butter.
7. Serve the roasted vegetables on top of the creamy polenta. Garnish with chopped basil.

Draw an illustration of Mrs. Sheff cooking.

"Create a home where the kitchen is at the center" ~ Mrs. Sheff

Little Lasagnas

These little veggie lasagnas are awesome for the whole family, parents included! The sauté of spinach and mushrooms give this dish a flavorful punch. Made with wontons and not pasta, they are unique and delicious! Serve them with a salad, or take them on-the-go for a quick and easy dinner that's simple and healthy. Try our recipe for Veggie Bolognese Sauce in this recipe.

Prep time: 15 minutes   **Total time:** 1 hour

Yields 12 servings

2-3 Tbsp. olive oil	1 ½ cups mozzarella cheese
1 pint mushrooms, *finely chopped*	Save ½ cup for topping
2 cups spinach, *sliced thin*	15 oz. ricotta cheese
36 wonton wrappers	4 cups tomato sauce
½ cups parmesan cheese	Top with fresh basil

Directions:

1. Preheat oven to 400°.

2. Spray a muffin pan with nonstick cooking spray.

3. Over medium heat, use a skillet to sauté the vegetables in olive oil until soft and fragrant. *Approximate time: 5 minutes.*

4. Combine parmesan, mozzarella and ricotta cheese in a small bowl, set aside. *(Note: remember to save ½ cup of the mozzarella for your topping!)*

5. Being layering your little lasagnas. Place one wonton square in a muffin pan.

6. Add some of the sautéed vegetables first, then add a spoonful of the cheese mixture and fresh tomato sauce. Top with a second wonton.

7. Continue layering **three times,** ending with the sauce. Top with remainder mozzarella cheese.

8. Bake for 20 minutes until hot and bubbly.

9. Garnish each little lasagna with basil and serve immediately.

Cookwork

What is bolognese sauce? What is usually in this tomato sauce?

_____

_____

_____

_____

_____

_____

_____

_____

"Magic happens in the kitchen." ~ Mrs. Sheff

Veggie Bolognese Sauce

Bolognese sauce is a magical sauce that is perfect for any shaped pasta or nestled in a lasagna. The vegetables give this tomato sauce a robust flavor that kids will adore! Serve with a sprinkle of parmesan cheese.

Prep time: 15 minutes   **Total time:** 1 hour

Yields 1 serving

2 Tbsp. olive oil
2 gloves garlic, *finely chopped*
1 small onion, *finely chopped*
3 carrots, *finely chopped*
3 stalks of celery, *finely chopped*

1 can crushed tomatoes
1 lb. rigatoni or cavatappi pasta
Parmesan cheese
1 pint of mushrooms, *finely chopped*

Directions:

1. Over medium heat in a large saucepan, add olive oil.
2. Sauté garlic, onion, carrot, celery and mushrooms for 5 min. until soft and fragrant.
3. Add a can of crushed tomatoes.
4. Boil the pasta according to the package directions.
5. Combine sauce with pasta and stir to combine.

Optional: 1 pound ground turkey, browned.

Cookwork

Do a little research on the history and types of soup.

_____

_____

_____

_____

_____

_____

_____

_____

"Cook. Eat. Nourish." ~ Mrs. Sheff

Rainbow Tortilla Soup

Cook up a big pot of this tortilla soup for a comforting and healthy meal. The flavors of the colorful mix of vegetables combine perfectly. Serve with crispy tortilla strips, chopped avocado and cheese. Everyone in your home will adore this meal.

Prep time: 15 minutes   **Total time:** 30 minutes

Yields 6 servings

2 Tbsp olive oil
1 small onion, *finely chopped*
1 poblano pepper, *finely chopped*
2 tsp. cumin
4 tomatillos
2 Tbsp cilantro, chopped
1 ~ 32 oz. box of chicken stock
1 ~ 8.5 oz can corn, *drained*
1 ~ 14.5 oz can of petite diced tomatoes

1 ~ 15 oz. can of reduced sodium black beans
2 whole wheat tortillas diced and 6 extra for strips or cups
Salt & pepper
Toppings:
Cheddar cheese
Sour cream
Diced avocado

Directions:

1. Over medium heat, add olive oil, onion and poblano pepper into a Dutch oven. Then season with salt & pepper and let sauté for 5 minutes until soft

2. Meanwhile puree the tomatillos and cilantro in food processor or blender. Add a splash of the chicken stock.

3. Add the puree to the Dutch oven and stir to combine.

4. Add rest of the chicken stock, corn, black beans and tomatoes.

5. Add diced tortillas to the soup as well. These will help to thicken the soup.

6. Bring to a boil and reduce heat. Then let soup simmer for 30 minutes.

Tortilla strips or cups
Cut tortillas into strips or circles. Place circles in a muffin pan. Spray with olive oil spray and bake at 350° for 10-15 minutes until golden brown.

Invent a new tool for eating spaghetti.

"Light candles for a special family meal." ~ Mrs. Sheff

Spaghetti with Turkey Meatballs

Spaghetti and meatballs has always been a family favorite. Twisting spaghetti using a fork and spoon always makes kids giggle. Serve up some family fun with these yummy turkey meatballs and spaghetti.

Prep time: 10 minutes   **Total time:** 1 hour

Yields 6-8 servings

4 Tbsp. olive oil	1 slice bread soaked in ½ cup milk
3 garlic cloves	1 egg
1 ~ 28 oz. can crushed tomatoes	¼ cup finely chopped parsley
1 Tbsp. fresh basil, *thinly sliced*	1 lb. whole wheat spaghetti
1 lb. ground turkey breast	Salt & pepper

Directions:

1. Combine ground turkey, bread, egg, parsley and a garlic clove grated. Season with salt & pepper.
2. Over medium heat, add 2 Tbsp. olive oil to a large sauté pan.
3. Form meatballs and add to the sauté pan.
4. Sauté the meatballs until cooked thoroughly. *Approximate time: 10 minutes.*
5. Meanwhile, over medium heat, add the remaining olive oil into a Dutch oven.
6. Add garlic and sauté until fragrant. *Approximate time: 3 minutes.*
7. Add can of crushed tomatoes, basil and season to taste.
8. Let sauce and meatballs simmer for 30 minutes together.
9. Cook pasta according to the package directions.
10. Toss pasta with the sauce and meatballs.

Cooking.
Magical.
Fun.

Draw Mrs. Sheff making Alphabet Soup.

"Nothing says comfort more that a bowl of soup." ~ *Mrs. Sheff*

*Cooking. Magical. Fun.

Page 42

Alphabet Soup

Alphabet Soup a delicious way to eat a rainbow of vegetables and have fun spelling silly words. A great healthy dish on a cold, snowy day! Serve with warm, crusty bread.

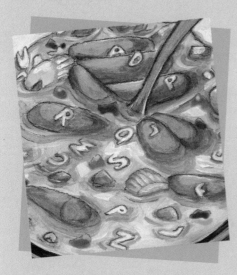

Prep time: 15 minutes   **Total time:** 45 minutes

Yields 8-10 servings

2 Tbsp. olive oil
1 garlic clove, *grated*
1 small onion, *finely chopped*
4 medium sized carrots,
   sliced on the diagonal
4 celery ribs, *diced*
2 zucchini, *diced*

1 ~ 14oz. can of petite diced tomatoes
2 cups baby spinach, *coarsely chopped*
1 ~ 32oz. box of chicken stock
1 cup alphabets pasta
½ cup parmesan cheese
Salt & pepper

Directions:

1. In a large stock pot, add olive oil and sauté the onion and garlic until fragrant. *Approximately 5 minutes*
2. Add carrots, celery, and zucchini and season with salt and pepper.
3. Continue sautéing for 10 additional minutes until veggies are soft.
4. Then add the box of chicken stock and diced tomatoes and bring back to a boil.
5. Next add pasta, stir and bring back to a boil.
6. Then reduce heat to medium and let simmer for 10 minutes until pasta is cooked.
7. Add chopped spinach and sprinkle with parmesan cheese.

Cooking.
Magical.
Fun.

Create your own Breakfast Burrito!

Ingredients

Prep time:___minutes   **Total time:**___minutes

Yields ____ servings

"Inspire children to be budding chefs." ~ Mrs. Sheff

Breakfast Burrito

Warm tortillas filled with scrabbled eggs and veggies for breakfast will start your day off right. Serve with fruit salad.

Prep time: 15 minutes   **Total time:** 30 minutes

Yields 6-8 servings

8 eggs, *scrambled*
1 cup chopped spinach
8 oz. fresh mushrooms, *sliced*
½ cup cheddar or Monterey Jack cheese
1 large tomato, *diced*

1 small onion, *finely chopped*
2 Tbsp cilantro
6-8 whole wheat tortillas
Salt & pepper

Directions:

1. Over medium-low heat, add butter to large skillet. Add spinach and mushrooms.
2. Then sauté until soft and season with salt & pepper. *Approximate time: 5 minutes.*
3. Meanwhile, add tomato, onion and cilantro to a food processor and process in short pulses until finely chopped but not puréed.
4. Reduce heat to low and remove vegetables from the skillet.
5. Then add eggs and stir slowly until cooked through. Season with salt & pepper and add cheese.
6. Make breakfast burritos by combining eggs, veggies and salsa and wrapping in a tortilla.

Cooking.
Magical.
Fun.

Search for Silly Chilli.

```
J  M  L  S  O  C  A  T  E  T  J  A  P  F
U  J  C  P  C  O  R  N  Q  J  Q  T  E  Y
S  D  L  I  O  S  I  A  D  E  Z  I  P  B
R  P  N  H  C  I  N  N  A  M  O  N  P  D
E  R  I  C  H  S  S  I  T  K  K  E  Q
B  A  I  Z  I  E  I  E  D  E  N  W  R  M
R  V  S  C  L  A  S  I  V  H  H  X  P  V
A  Z  B  H  I  S  I  L  B  I  N  D  E  R
D  N  Q  I  T  O  L  I  N  A  L  U  V  Y
D  O  Y  C  C  N  L  H  S  Z  K  O  W  I
E  P  D  K  E  I  Y  C  V  B  W  E  Z  Y
H  U  Y  E  W  N  Z  J  O  Y  C  L  D  L
C  T  J  N  P  G  U  V  J  N  E  E  R  G
M  K  C  O  T  S  F  S  V  R  F  M  A  H
```

Baked	Silly	Chili
Cheddar	Pepper	Cinnamon
Oil	Chilies	Stock
Chicken	Seasoning	Corn
Olive	Chips	Taco

Silly Chili

What makes this chili so silly? It is the cinnamon which gives this chili a very unique twist. Swirl in some sour cream and top with some cheddar cheese and serve with baked tortilla cups.

Prep time: 15 minutes   **Total time:** 45 minutes

Yields 4-6 servings

2 Tbsp. olive oil
2 boneless and skinless chicken breasts, *cooked*
2 green peppers, *diced*
1 small onion, chopped
1 can chopped green chilies

2 tsp. cinnamon
1 Tbsp. taco seasoning
1 cup corn fresh or frozen
1 ~ 32 oz. box chicken stock
8 oz. cheddar cheese, *shredded*

Directions:
1. Bring 4 cups water to a boil and add chicken breasts. Reduce heat and let simmer for 25-30 minutes.
2. Meanwhile in a stockpot over medium heat, add olive oil and sauté onion, green pepper and chillies until soft.
3. Add cinnamon, taco seasoning and corn and reduce heat.
4. Shred chicken and add to the pot along with chicken stock and bring to a boil.
5. Reduce heat and let simmer for 30 minutes.

Cookwork

Brainstorm a list of fruit smoothies.

_____

_____

_____

_____

_____

_____

_____

_____

_____

"Go to a local farm and pick your own produce." ~ Mrs. Sheff

Yummy Smoothies

Start a winter morning off with a delicious tropical smoothie. Mango, banana, and orange juice will take you away to a sunny beach in the tropics even on a cold morning. Try adding in pineapple for an even sunnier drink. Juicing has become so popular. It is a great way to get your children to eat their veggies. Try the Green Goody juice! It also tastes like a tropical smoothie drink!

Orange You Delicious!

Prep time: 5 minutes   **Total time:** 10 minutes

Yields 1 serving

1 banana
½ cup frozen mango
½ cup orange juice

½ cup low-fat milk
1 cup vanilla Greek yogurt

Directions:
1. In a small blender, add in all of the ingredients and combine until well blended.

Green Goody Juice

Prep time: 5 minutes   **Total time:** 10 minutes

Yields 1 serving

1 banana
½ apple
1½ cup pineapple

½ cup spinach leaves
½ water

Directions:
1. Blend all of the ingredients in a small blender with a little ice.

Cooking.
Magical.
Fun.

Write notes about making this recipe.

"Bring a home cooked meal to a local soup kitchen." ~ Mrs. Sheff

Tuscan Soup

This hearty soup is very delicious! It is a simple weeknight meal to create on a winter day. Serve with a crusty baguette and a sprinkle of parmesan cheese.

Prep time: 15 minutes   **Total time:** 45 minutes

Yields 6-8 servings

2 Tbsp extra-virgin olive oil
2 garlic cloves, *finely chopped*
1 small onion, *finely chopped*
3 carrots, *sliced on the diagonal*
4 celery ribs, *sliced on the diagonal*
2 Tbsp. tomato paste

1 can cannellini beans, drained & rinsed
2 cups kale or spinach, thinly sliced
½ cup small pasta, such as ditallini
1 ~ 32 oz. box of chicken stock
Parmesan cheese
Salt & pepper

Directions:

1. In a large stock pot, add olive oil over medium heat.
2. Add onion and garlic and sauté for two minutes.
3. Add carrots and celery and continue sautéing for 10 minutes.
4. Season with salt and pepper.
5. Add box of stock and tomato paste and bring to a boil.
6. Add beans and kale and bring to a boil.
7. Add pasta, stir and bring back to a boil.
8. Reduce heat to medium and let simmer for 15 minutes.

Cooking.
Magical.
Fun.

Cookwork

What is the history of a chicken pot pie?

_____

_____

_____

_____

_____

_____

_____

_____

"Make a pot of homemade chicken soup." ~ Mrs. Sheff

Mini-Chicken Pot Pies

Chicken pot pie is a wonderful comforting meal for families. Make them miniature and you have added in tons of fun. Puff pastry is a splendid topping for the little pot pies. Watch as these disappear!

Prep time: 15 minutes   **Total time:** 1 hour

Yields 8-10 servings

3 Tbsp. flour
3 Tbsp. butter
2 cups low-fat milk
3 carrots, *diced*
3 stalks of celery, *diced*
1 small onion, *finely chopped*
2 potatoes, *diced and cooked*

½ cup frozen peas
2 chicken breasts, cooked and diced
1 tsp. fresh thyme, chopped
Salt & pepper
1 package puff pastry
1 egg

Directions:

1. Preheat oven to 400°. Set out puff pastry to thaw, and then cut 8 squares of puff pastry and set aside.

2. Peel and dice 2 potatoes and place in 2 cups of cold water. Bring water to a boil and let cook until tender. *Approximate time: 10-12 minutes.*

3. Meanwhile melt butter in a saucepan over low heat. Add flour and using a whisk combine with the melted butter. Add milk in slowly over medium heat and whisk until combined. Season sauce with salt and pepper to taste. Turn heat to low and set aside.

4. Then over medium heat in a large sauté pan, sauté the onion, carrot, celery and chopped fresh thyme. Season with salt and pepper and let cook 10 minutes.

5. Add chicken and sauce and stir to combine until heated through completely.

6. Add in peas at the end so that they remain bright green.

7. Spoon mixture into one large pie pan or 8-10 mini pie pans.

8. Top each pot pie with the squares of puff pastry and brush with an egg wash.
   (1 egg plus 2 tablespoons water whisked together)

9. Bake pot pies for 15 minutes.

Cooking.
Magical.
Fun.

Create your own wintry recipe.

Ingredients

Prep time:___minutes   **Total time:**___minutes

Yields ____ servings

"Cook and eat together as a family" ~ Mrs. Sheff

Pizza!

Making your own pizza is such a fun family adventure. Everybody can even make their own individual pies and have a pizza party! Serve with a variety of toppings to make every pizza unique. Want to add a twist? Make white pizzas that look like little snowmen!

Prep time: 15 minutes   **Total time:** 90 minutes

Yields 2 large pizzas or 8 mini pies

1 ¼ cups of warm water
2 Tbsp. olive oil
1 package rapid rise yeast
2+ cups of bread flour
1 cup white whole wheat flour

2 tsp. salt
Toppings:
 Green pepper
 Mushrooms
 Caramelized onions

Directions:

1. Place water, olive oil and yeast in a liquid measure cup and let rest for 10 minutes to activate the yeast.
2. In a stand mixer fitted with dough hook, place flours and salt.
3. Add water mixture to the flour slowly.
4. Allow to knead for 5 minutes and add flour as needed.
5. Place in a warm spot and allow to rise for at least one hour.
6. Punch down and let dough rest for 5 minutes.
7. Create your pizza masterpiece.
8. Bake pizza at 450° for 10-12 minutes.

- Mrs. Sheff's -
Spring Recipes

Spring Pasta

Curlicue pasta topped with green sauce! Your kids will fall head over heals with this fast and delicious spring meal. Serve with crusty bread and a garden salad.

Prep time: 10 minutes   **Total time:** 20 minutes

Yields 8 servings

1 lb. rotini pasta
½ cup cooked pasta water
2 Tbsp. olive oil
6 scallions, *finely sliced*

1 bag frozen peas, *defrosted*
  or 2 cups fresh peas
1 Tbsp. fresh parsley, *chopped*
½ cup parmesan cheese

Directions:

1. Cook pasta according to package directions. Reserve ½ cup of water.

2. Over medium heat, sauté scallions in olive oil until soft and fragrant. *Approximate time: 5 minutes.*

3. Purée ½ bag of peas in food processor or blender. Then, add parsley and blend well.

4. Combine scallions, pea purée, remaining peas and reserved pasta water. Toss with pasta.

5. Sprinkle with parmesan cheese and serve.

Cooking.
Magical.
Fun.

Cookwork

What are some other healthy types of pancakes?

_____

_____

_____

_____

_____

_____

_____

_____

_____

"Grow up learning to cook and love healthy food." ~ Mrs. Sheff

Lemon Blueberry Pancakes

This winning combination of blueberries and lemon make an ordinary pancake extraordinary. Serve with plain or vanilla yogurt. Pure maple syrup also pairs beautifully with these delicious pancakes.

new pic needed

Prep time: 10 minutes   **Total time:** 30 minutes

Yields 8 servings

1 lemon, *juiced*
1 ½ cups low fat milk
1 ½ cups whole grain white flour
¼ tsp. salt
1 Tbsp. baking powder

3 Tbsp. raw cane sugar
1 large egg
1 ½ tsp. vanilla extract
1 cup blueberries
Maple syrup, *warmed*

Directions:

1. In a large bowl, combine flour, salt, baking powder and sugar.

2. In seperate bowl, whisk egg into milk and add vanilla.

3. Add lemon juice to milk mixture and stir to combine.

4. Add wet mixture to dry ingredients.

5. Then, gently fold in blueberries.

6. Heat a heavy griddle or skillet over medium heat and spray with cooking spray.

7. Drop batter into pan and cook on both sides until golden brown.

8. Stack pancakes and top with maple syrup.

Cookwork

Search for other ways to wrap up a dumpling.

Where do wontons come from?

"Fill you home with yummy scents of a cooking or baking." ~ *Mrs. Sheff*

The New Dainty Dumplings

This new version of a Cooking's Cool favorite is a perfect combination of carrots, celery, spinach and onion with a blend of brown rice and quinoa. Not only are they fun to wrap up but delicious and nutritious!

Prep time: 45 minutes   **Total time:** 1 hour

Yields 8 servings

2 Tbsp. canola oil
2 carrots
3 stalks of celery
1 cup fresh spinach, *chopped*
1 small onion
1 cup brown rice & red quinoa blend

½ tsp. garlic powder
1 package wonton wrappers (48)
Salt & pepper
Dipping Sauce:
¼ cup soy sauce
1 Tbsp. honey

Directions:

1. Whisk soy sauce and honey. Set aside.

2. Cook brown rice and quinoa blend according to package directions.

3. Meanwhile, in a food processor, finely chop carrots, celery, spinach and onion.

4. Add canola oil to saucepan over medium heat. Sauté the vegetables until soft. Season with garlic powder, salt and pepper.

5. Transfer above mixture into medium size bowl. Add rice and quinoa blend. Let stand and cool.

6. Add 1 tsp. filling to the center of each wonton.

7. Paint edges of wontons with water. Fold into triangle and bring side corners to top. Press and seal with water.

8. Bake or steam wontons. Serve with dipping sauce.

*Bake: at 375° on a cookie sheet lined with foil for 10 minutes. Brush each dumpling with canola or olive oil before baking.
*Steam: In a bamboo steamer or a saucepan fitted with a steam basket over medium heat for 5 minutes.

Cooking.
Magical.
Fun.

Write notes about making this recipe.

_____

_____

_____

_____

_____

_____

_____

_____

_____

_____

"""Magic happens in the kitchen." ~ Mrs. Sheff

Quinoa Spring Rolls

Kids love to make these spring rolls wrapping up fresh veggies and quinoa. These rolls are a delicious way to celebrate spring.

Prep time: 10 minutes   **Total time:** 30 minutes

Yields 8 servings

1 cucumber, cut into julienne strips
2 carrots, peeled and cut
2 cups baby spinach
½ cup quinoa, cooked
12 rice paper wrappers

Dipping Sauce:
 ¼ cup soy sauce
 2 Tbsp. honey
 1 tsp. sesame oil

Directions:

1. Whisk soy sauce, honey and sesame oil together in a small bowl. Set aside for dipping.
2. Cook quinoa according to package directions.
3. Dip rice paper wrapper into water for 15-20 seconds, until pliable. Work with one at a time.
4. Lay the rice paper on a towel and layer with spinach, carrots and cucumber. Add 2 Tbsp. quinoa.
5. Wrap and roll each tightly.
6. Repeat with all of the remaining rice paper wrappers.

Draw an illustration of your own garden.

"Great joy is found harvesting a garden that you planted." ~ Mrs. Sheff

Spring Vegetable Soup

Soup in the spring? Try this simple soup for supper during the spring with your family. The fresh, spring vegetables are absolute stars in this soup.

Prep time: 15 minutes   **Total time:** 35 minutes

Yields 6 servings

2 Tbsp. olive oil
1 clove garlic
1 bunch scallions, *finely chopped*
2 carrots, *diced*
32 oz. box of chicken stock
1 chicken breast, *cooked and shredded*

1 bunch asparagus, *cut*
1 cup fresh or frozen peas
½ cup thin spaghetti, *broken*
¼ fresh parsley, *chopped*

Directions:

1. In a stockpot over medium heat, sauté garlic and scallions until soft and fragrant. *Approximate time: 5 minutes.*

2. Add diced carrot and asparagus and sauté an additional 5 minutes.

3. Add chicken stock and bring to a boil.

4. Add pasta and reduce heat to medium until pasta is cooked according to package directions.

5. Add chicken, peas and parsley at the last minute and heat through.

6. Serve immediately and top with a sprinkle of parmesan cheese.

Cooking.
Magical.
Fun.

Create your own afternoon snack.

Ingredients

Prep time:___minutes   **Total time:**___minutes

Yields ____ servings

"Raw veggies and fruit make great snacks." ~ Mrs. Sheff

Fruit Pizzas

Fruit Pizzas are a wonderful way to dress up a pancake. They make weekend pancake breakfasts fun simply by adding a colorful mix of fresh fruit to a whole wheat pancake. Pizza has never been more delicious!

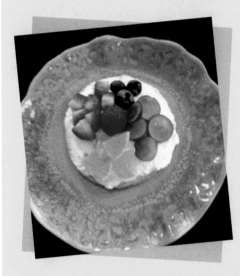

Prep time: 15 minutes   **Total time:** 45 minutes

Yields 12 servings • 1 fruit pizza per serving

1 ½ cups low-fat milk
1 ½ cup whole wheat flour
¼ teaspoon salt
1 Tbsp. baking powder
3 Tbsp. raw sugar
1 large egg
2 tsp. vanilla extract
1 pint heavy cream
3 Tbsp. honey

Whipped Topping:
 1 pint heavy cream
 3 Tbsp. honey
Toppings:
 Strawberries, *sliced*
 Kiwi, *sliced*
 Blueberries
 Mandarin orange sections

Directions:

1. In a large bowl, combine flour, salt, baking powder and sugar.
2. Whisk an egg into the milk and add vanilla.
3. Add the wet mixture to dry ingredients.
4. Heat a heavy griddle or skillet over medium heat and spray lightly with cooking spray.
5. Pour batter on to the griddle. Flip and cook on both sides until golden brown.
6. Meanwhile, using and electric mixer, whip pint of heavy cream until peaks form. *Approximate time: 3 minutes.* Add heavy cream and combine until smooth.
7. Spread whipped topping on the pancakes.
8. Top with a colorful mix of fresh fruit.

Cooking. *Magical.* Fun.

Search for Petite Pita Pizzas.

```
Y V F O T G P E V I L O B Q Q
J T I G O W E J C F B Q K M F
U M N X M A T L T O S H O R N
A S W K A B I I C R A Z E P V
S T B J T A T F E S Z S Y W U
R L I E O K E P E A H D G D I
U G R P E E P V R S P X Y S Q
D A D P S E A E M N X L E U C
F R O I P E L O S B B Y C R M
B L U Z L L O O C B E F U O R
O I R Z A R W A U W U S J B T
S C O A H D C B B J H I A A T
U P G S Z R D K C E U S E W K
W X U L W M V F D D I H O I L
E M E L O H W W N L W F G W P
```

Bake	Crushed	Leaves
Oil	Petite	Tomatoes
Basil	Fresh	Mozzarella
Olive	Pita	Wheat
Bubbly	Garlic	Mushrooms
Peppers	Pizzas	Whole

Petite Pita Pizzas

Ever had pizza on a pita? They are the perfect crunchy crust for a Margherita pizza with a chiffonade of fresh basil on the top. Want to make your pizza even healthier? Then try our Veggie Bolognese Sauce on your pizza!

Prep time: 15 minutes   **Total time:** 45 minutes

Yields 6 servings • 1 petite pizza per serving

2 Tbsp. olive oil
2 cloves garlic, *finely chopped*
1 ~ 28 oz. can crushed tomatoes
½ cup fresh basil, *thinly sliced*
8 oz. fresh mozzarella, *sliced*

6 whole wheat pitas
½ cup water
Salt & pepper
Toppings:
  Green pepper
  Mushrooms

Directions:

1. Preheat oven to 450°.

2. Over medium heat, add olive oil to a medium saucepan.

3. Add garlic and sauté until fragrant. *Approximate time: 3 minutes.*

4. Add crushed tomatoes and water to the sauce.

5. Season with salt and pepper and let simmer for 30 minutes.

6. Meanwhile, slice each pita in half to form two rounds.

7. Bake the pitas until slightly browned. *Approximate time: 5 minutes.*

8. Top each pita with sauce, cheese and vegetable toppings.

9. Bake until golden brown and bubbly. *Approximate time: 10 minutes.*

Cooking.
Magical.
Fun.

Create your own wrap.

Ingredients

Prep time: ___minutes **Total time:** ___minutes

Yields ____ servings

"Start a cookbook collection." ~ Mrs. Sheff

Rainbow Wraps

Wrap up a rainbow of colorful vegetables for a tasty snack or lunch. They are perfect for a healthy lunch for school. Just add some fruit and water to your child's lunch box.

Prep time: 15 minutes   **Total time:** 45 minutes

Yields 6 servings

6 whole wheat or spinach tortillas
8 oz. cream cheese
1 Tbsp. taco seasoning
1 avocado, *mashed*
3 carrots, *thinly sliced*

3 cucumbers, *thinly sliced*
3 celery stalks, *thinly sliced*
3 green peppers, *thinly sliced*
1 head Romaine lettuce

Directions:

1. In a small bowl, combine cream cheese, taco seasoning and mashed avocado.

2. Lay one tortilla flat and spread with cream cheese mixture.

3. Place one lettuce leaf on the tortilla and arrange thinly sliced vegetables inside.

4. Roll the tortilla up and slice in little pinwheels.

Cooking.
Magical.
Fun.

Design a produce market full of baskets and bins.

filled with a variety of colorful fruit and vegetables.
Add a special scale and cash register to your illustration.

"Join a Community Share Agriculture in your community." ~ Mrs. Sheff

Rainbow Frittata

This frittata is a yummy mix of colorful peppers and onions. Serve with warm blueberry muffins and fruit salad.

Prep time: 15 minutes   **Total time:** 45 minutes

Yields 6 servings

1 Tbsp. olive oil
1 small onion, *diced*
1 green pepper, *diced*
1 orange pepper, *diced*

1 yellow pepper, *diced*
12 eggs, *beaten well*
3 potatoes, *peeled, cubed and cooked*
1 cup cheddar cheese, *shredded*

Directions:

1. Preheat oven to 375°.

2. Over medium heat, sauté the onion and peppers in olive oil in an oven-safe skillet.

3. Then season the vegetables with salt & pepper and cook for 5 minutes until soft.

4. Boil peeled and cubed potatoes for 10 minutes in salted water.

5. Add eggs and potatoes back in skillet and stir to combine over medium heat. Continue stirring over low heat until curds begin to appear. *Approximate time: 5 minutes.*

6. Bake in oven for about 15-20 minutes until top is set and golden brown.

7. Make mini frittatas! Place diced potatoes in each spot in a muffin pan. Pour eggs in each spot and add vegetables to the top. Bake for 15-20 minutes.

Draw your own burger with yummy toppings.

"Find the joy of cooking and eating healthy." ~ *Mrs. Sheff*

Chicken Caesar Burgers

If you like Caesar salad, you will love these burgers. Made with the flavors of this scrumptious salad the taste of these burgers resembles the flavor of this classic recipe.

Prep time: 15 minutes   **Total time:** 45 minutes

Yields 4-6 servings

2 garlic cloves, *finely chopped*
¼ cup parsley, *finely chopped*
2 Tbsp. Dijon mustard
Dash of Worcestershire sauce
½ cup panko breadcrumbs
Salt & pepper

1 lb ground chicken
2 Tbsp. olive oil
1 head Romaine lettuce
Caesar salad dressing
4-6 whole wheat buns

Directions:

1. Combine the first four ingredients in a large bowl.

2. Form mixture into 4-6 burgers.

3. Coat each burger with panko breadcrumbs.

4. Sauté in skillet over medium heat with olive oil until completely cooked through and brown. *Approximate time:* 5 minutes per side.

5. Meanwhile chop lettuce into thin strips and toss with Caesar dressing.

6. Serve salad on top of burger on bun.

Cooking.
Magical.
Fun.

Create your own spring recipe.

Ingredients

Prep time:___minutes **Total time:**___minutes

Yields ____ servings

"The best days are the ones that end with a comforting meal." ~ Mrs. Sheff

Mini Turkey Burgers

Make these little turkey burgers for your next party! Your guests can add their favorite toppings. Everyone will have a ball creating their own burgers. Serve with a big garden salad.

Prep time: 15 minutes   **Total time:** 45 minutes

Yields 12 servings

2 Tbsp. olive oil
1 small onion, *grated*
1 green pepper, *finely chopped*
2 Tbsp. cilantro or parsley, *finely chopped*
1 Tbsp. cumin
1 lb. ground turkey breast

Salt & pepper
Toppings:
  Lettuce
  Tomato
  Sliced onion
  Guacamole

Directions:

1. Over medium heat in a skillet, add olive oil, onion and pepper.

2. Sauté the vegetables for 5 minutes until soft and fragrant. Set aside to cool.

3. Then combine ground turkey with the cooled onions, peppers and cilantro or parsley.

4. Shape into miniature-sized burgers.

5. Over medium heat, sauté the burgers in a skillet or grill.
   Approximate time: 6-7 min. per side until cooked thoroughly.

6. Place 1 slice of Monterey Jack, pepper jack or cheddar cheese on burgers and let cook for an additional 2 minutes until cheese is melted.

7. Place on miniature whole wheat buns.

- Mrs. Sheff's -
Summer Recipes

BBQ Chicken Sandwiches

These sweet and savory pulled chicken sandwiches are a perfect dish to serve at your next barbecue. Kids will adore the homemade sauce and the colorful slaw mix.

Prep time: 15 minutes   **Total time:** 1.5 hours

Yields 8 servings

2 boneless, skinless chicken breasts, *cooked and shredded*
6 Tbsp. olive oil
1 small onion, *chopped finely*
1 clove garlic, *grated*
1 cup ketchup
3 Tbsp. brown sugar

1 Tbsp. Worcestershire sauce
½ head green cabbage
½ head red cabbage
2 carrots
½ cup olive oil mayonnaise
3 Tbsp. red wine vinegar
Salt & pepper

Directions:

1. Shred cabbage, grate carrots and set aside.

2. Whisk red wine vinegar and mayonnaise together until well combined.

3. Slowly whisk in 4 tablespoons of olive oil. Season with salt and pepper.

4. Combine dressing with the slaw mix and refrigerate for at least one hour.

5. Over medium heat, sauté the onion and garlic in the remaining 2 tablespoons of olive oil until soft and fragrant. *Approximate time: 5 minutes.*

6. Add ketchup, brown sugar and Worcestershire sauce. Season with salt and pepper.

7. Simmer barbeque sauce on low heat. *Approximate time: 30 minutes.*

8. Combine shredded chicken with barbeque sauce.

9. Place pulled barbeque chicken on a whole wheat bun. Top with slaw mix.

Cooking.
Magical.
Fun.

Cookwork

Search for the ingredients in a traditional Caprese salad.

_____

_____

_____

_____

_____

_____

_____

_____

_____

"Experiment with new foods or recipes." ~ Mrs. Sheff

Caprese Pasta Salad

Pasta, basil, tomatoes and mozzarella cheese are always a perfect combination. Add in cucumbers and olives to create a pasta salad that is both tasty and crunchy.

Prep time: 15 minutes   **Total time:** 1 hour

Yields 6 servings

1 lb. whole grain pasta
½ pint red grape tomatoes
½ pint yellow grape tomatoes
1 container fresh mozzarella bocconcini or
   1 ball fresh mozzarella, *cubed*
½ cup basil, *thinly sliced*

1 small can of olives, *sliced*
1 cucumber, *diced*
Dressing
2 cloves garlic, *chopped finely*
¼ cup basalmic vinegar
¾ cup olive oil

Directions:

1. Cook pasta according to package directions.
2. Prepare dressing by combining olive oil, vinegar and garlic in a mason jar. Shake well.
3. Combine pasta with diced vegetables, mozzarella cheese and basil.
4. Toss pasta salad with dressing and season with salt and pepper. Refrigerate for at least an hour before serving.

Draw **Mrs. Sheff preparing kabobs.**

"Take time to enjoy a Sunday meal." ~ Mrs. Sheff

Citrus Chicken Kabobs

The three citrus marinade makes these kabobs! Children love to eat kabobs especially when they taste like a fajita! Serve with warm tortillas, brown rice and salsa.

Prep time: 15 minutes   **Total time:** 90 minutes

Yields 6 kabobs

4 skinless, boneless chicken breasts
2 Tbsp. olive oil
1 Tbsp. lime juice
1 Tbsp. lemon juice
1 Tbsp. orange juice
1 tsp. chili powder
1 tsp. cumin

½ tsp. garlic powder
¼ tsp. salt
¼ tsp. pepper
1 green pepper, *cut into squares*
1 orange pepper, *cut into squares*
1 red pepper, *cut into squares*
1 red onion, *cut into squares*

Directions:

1. Preheat the grill for high heat and brush with oil.

2. Clean chicken and pat dry with paper towels.

3. Cut chicken into 2 inch pieces.

4. Place all ingredients (#2-9) for marinade in a resealable bag.

5. Place chicken in bag and let marinate for at least but no more than one hour.

6. Thread chicken, peppers and onions onto skewers. Note: If using wood skewers, presoak them to prevent burning on grill.

7. Grill kabobos until chicken is cooked thoroughly. *Approximate time: 15 minutes.*

Draw **your plate filled with Confetti Nachos.**

"Comforting cooking sparks a love of food." ~ Mrs. Sheff

Confetti Nachos

All kids love to eat nachos. What makes these nachos unique? It's the yummy cheese sauce! Top blue corn chips with colorful toppings to make these a guaranteed family favorite.

Prep time: 10 minutes   **Total time:** 30 minutes

Yields 8 servings

3 Tbsp. all-purpose flour
3 Tbsp. butter
2 cups low-fat milk
2 cups low-fat cheddar cheese
Salt & pepper
Bag of blue corn tortilla chips
1 can low sodium black beans,
  drained and rinsed

1 tomato, *diced*
6 scallions, *sliced on the bias*
1 head Romaine lettuce, *thinly sliced*
Toppings:
  Guacamole
  Low-fat sour cream
  Fresh salsa

Directions:
1. Preheat oven to 400°.
2. In medium saucepan over medium heat, melt butter and add flour. Cook for 1 minute sirring constantly.
3. Slowly whisk the milk into the pan and season with salt and pepper. Whisk until smooth.
4. Reduce the heat to low and add cheese. Stir until melted.
5. Arrange tortilla chips on baking sheet. Top with cheese sauce, black beans, tomato, lettuce and scallions. Bake until chips are browned and crispy. *Approximate time: 10 minutes.*
6. Top with salsa, sour cream and guacamole.

Cooking.
Magical.
Fun.

Cookwork

What is the history behind s'mores?

_____

_____

_____

_____

_____

_____

_____

_____

"Treats should be eaten in moderation." ~ Mrs. Sheff

Raspberry S'mores

The s'more could quite possibly be the perfect dessert for kids with chocolate, marshmallows and graham crackers. This variation combines white chocolate, mini marshmallows and raspberries. Make individual s'mores or serve as a s'more dip.

Prep time: 10 minutes   **Total time:** 20 minutes

Yields 8 servings

1 bag white chocolate chips, *melted*
1 bag small marshmallows
2 pints fresh raspberries

Directions:

1. Preheat oven broiler.

2. Melt whole bag of chocolate chips in a microwave-safe bowl. Cook for 25 seconds on high. Stir and microwave for additional 25 seconds. Repeat until chocolate is melted and smooth.

3. In an oven safe casserole, layer the melted chocolate, fresh raspberries and top with marshmallows.

4. Place under the broiler until marshmallows are golden brown. *Approximate time: 3-5 minutes.*

5. Serve with toasted graham crackers.

Draw how to stuff and wrap a dumpling.

"Visit local produce stands." ~ Mrs. Sheff

Dainty Dumplings

The delicious little dumplings are a kid-tested and approved. Wrapping them up is half of the fun. Make these for a fun-filled family cooking adventure. Not only are they fun to wrap up, but they are delicious and nutritious, too!

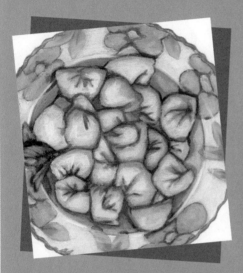

Prep time: 30 minutes **Total time:** 1 hour

Yields 6 servings

2 Tbsp. canola oil
2 chicken breasts, *cooked*
2 carrots
3 stalks of celery
1 small onion
½ tsp. garlic powder

1 package 50 wonton wrappers
Salt & pepper
Dipping Sauce:
 ¼ cup soy sauce
 1 Tbsp. honey

Directions:

1. Preheat oven to 375° to bake wontons.
2. In a food processor, finely chop the chicken and remove. Then finely chop the carrots, celery and onion.
3. Over medium heat, add canola oil and sauté the vegetables until soft and fragrant.
4. Add chicken, garlic powder and salt & pepper to taste and transfer to a medium sized bowl.
5. Add ½ teaspoon filling to each wonton.
6. Shape wontons as desired and seal with water.
7. Bake or steam wontons. Serve with dipping sauce ~ Enjoy!

Bake wontons at 375 degrees on a cookie sheet lined with foil for 10 minutes. Brush each dumpling lightly with canola oil or olive oil before baking. Steam wontons over medium heat on the stove using a steam rack in a medium sized saucepan ~ 5 minutes.

Cooking. *Magical.* Fun.

Search for Fruity Kabobs.

```
K P P H O N E Y Y F M Z Z Q I
J W N F H H X O W O N I W I K
P L L U F R O L O C G B V O O
A E P I C E H G U V L U X J D
F M A L T L G G A A Q S R H Y
V O T F F P T W C E E Z O T R
A N T F U P S K D P E O F U R
N Z E E A A B N A U L O R W E
I E R C B E X R P O Z P U I B
L S N A R N G M C L D V I X W
L T D R H I J A F A F L T B A
A L I E M P X N W T Q M Y Y R
E E X G R R U Q O N J X T J T
S S K E W E R S Y A L O C P S
A S B O B A K G D C M B V M Y
```

Blackberries	Pineapple	Honey
Lemon Zest	Fruity	Vanilla
Cantaloupe	Skewers	Kabobs
Pattern	Grapes	Yogurt
Colorful	Strawberry	Kiwi

Fruity Kabobs

Fruity Kabobs are a swirl of fun for children. They love to mix up fruit in colorful patterns. Watch as they magically disappear.

Prep time: 20 minutes   **Total time:** 20 minutes

Yields 12 servings

1 pint strawberries, *halved*	1 pint blackberries
2 cups purple grapes	1 8oz. container vanilla greek yogurt
1 cantaloupe, *cubed*	1 tsp. honey
1 pineapple, *cubed*	1 tsp. lemon zest
4 kiwi, *peeled and diced*	12 wooden skewers

Directions:

1. Skewer fruit in a colorful pattern.

2. Combine yogurt, honey and lemon zest.

3. Dip fruity kabobs in the yogurt dip.

Cooking.
Magical.
Fun.

Write notes about making this recipe.

_____

_____

_____

_____

_____

_____

_____

_____

_____

_____

_____

"Go on colorful food shopping sprees." ~ Mrs. Sheff

Schoolyard Salad

This pasta salad is perfect in the summer with fresh cucumbers, tomatoes, carrots, celery and peppers. Add whole wheat or whole grain pasta shaped in bow ties or shells. Then mix up a homemade vinaigrette for a superb dressing.

Prep time: 15 minutes **Total time:** 1 hour

Yields 8-10 servings

1 lb. whole grain pasta
3 carrots, *peeled and diced*
2 cucumbers, *diced*
3 stalks of celery, *diced*
2 green peppers, *diced*
1 pint grape tomatoes

¾ cup olive oil
¼ cup vinegar
1 garlic clove, *finely chopped*
1 Tbsp. mustard
Salt & pepper

Directions:

1. Cook pasta according to package directions.
2. Dice all of vegetables and place in a large bowl.
3. Place olive oil, vinegar, mustard, garlic in a mason jar and shake to combine.
4. Combine pasta, vegetables, and dressing in the large bowl.
   Chill pasta salad for one hour before serving.

Cookwork

Design your very own Berry Good Salad.

_____

_____

_____

_____

_____

_____

_____

_____

"Stock your kitchen with the tools of a chef." ~ Mrs. Sheff

Berry Good Salad

Salads made with a mix of fruits and vegetables are delicious. Try adding a mix of berries to your salads. It is the perfect mix of zesty and sweet!

Prep time: 15 minutes   **Total time:** 30 minutes

Yields 4 servings

1 bag fresh mesclun salad mix
1 cucumber, *diced*
1 pint up blueberries
½ pint strawberries, *sliced*
¼ cup sunflower seeds
½ cup feta cheese

Salt & pepper
Vinaigrette Dressing:
 ¾ cup olive oil
 ¼ white vinegar
 Juice from 1 lemon

Directions:

1. Prepare dressing by combining olive oil, vinegar, and lemon juice in a mason jar and shake to combine.

2. Place all fruit, vegetables, sunflower seeds and feta cheese in a salad bowl.

3. Add dressing and toss to combine.

Cooking.
Magical.
Fun.

Search for how to properly use chopsticks.

_____

_____

_____

_____

_____

_____

_____

_____

_____

_____

"Plan your weekly menus for the week." ~ Mrs. Sheff

Rainbow Noodle Bowls

Noodle bowls are a fun way to eat a rainbow of vegetables. The combination of colors make this dish beautiful and simply scrumptious. Serve with chopsticks!

Prep time: 15 minutes **Total time:** 30 minutes

Yields 4-6 servings

2 Tbsp. canola oil
2 cups broccoli florets
2 carrots, *thinly sliced*
2 cloves garlic, *finely chopped*
1 pint baby portabella mushrooms, *sliced*
1 red pepper, *thinly sliced*
1 lb. whole grain pasta, *cooked*

or 3 packs noodlicious pasta without seasoning
3 Tbsp. low sodium soy sauce
1 tsp. sesame oil
1 Tbsp. hoisin sauce
Garnish with green onions, *chopped on the bias*

Directions:

1. Cook pasta according to package directions.
2. Over medium-low heating a sauté, sauté garlic and mushrooms in canola oil.
3. Turn the heat to medium and add carrots, broccoli and red pepper and stir fry. *Approximate time: 5 min.*
4. Season with soy sauce, sesame oil and hoisin sauce.
5. Add cooked pasta and stir to combine.

Design your own unique pizza.

"Make homemade pizza at least once a week." ~ Mrs. Sheff

Crispy Caprese Pizza

Feast on this rustic pizza at your family table. Combine fresh mozzarella, summer tomatoes and basil on a homemade or ready-made pizza crust. Serve with an antipasti salad.

Prep time: 15 minutes   **Total time:** 90 minutes

Yields 1-2 pizzas

1 pint grape or heirloom tomatoes, *diced*
1 ball fresh mozzarella
½ cup fresh basil, *thinly sliced*
½ cup mozzarella cheese, *grated*
½ cup parmesan cheese

Crust:
1 ¼ cups of warm water
2 Tbsp. olive oil
1 package rapid rise yeast
2+ cups of bread flour
1 cup white whole wheat flour
2 tsp. salt

Directions:
1. Place water, olive oil and yeast in a liquid measure cup.
2. In a stand mixer fitted with dough hook, place flours and salt.
3. Add water mixture to the flour slowly.
4. Allow to knead for 5 minutes and add flour as needed.
5. Place in a warm spot and allow to rise for at least one hour.
6. Punch down and let dough rest for 5 minutes.
7. Roll pizza out into a large circle or rectangle and place on cookie sheet.
8. Create your pizza masterpiece by adding the tomatoes, cheese and basil.
9. Bake pizza at 450° for 10-12 minutes until golden brown and crispy.

Cookwork

What is the history of the Caesar salad?

_____

_____

_____

_____

_____

_____

_____

_____

"Take time each day to prepare a healthy meal." ~ Mrs. Sheff

Chicken Caesar Sandwhiches

Wrap up a delicious Caesar Salad in a tortilla! Make your own flavorful dressing and toss with chicken and vegetables. Serve with baked chips or a warm bowl of soup.

● **Prep time:** 30 minutes   **Total time:** 45 minutes ●

Yields 4-6 sandwhiches

1 small garlic clove, grated
1 Tbsp. Dijon mustard
1 cup light sour cream
Juice of ½ lemon
Dash of Worcestershire sauce
2 Tbsp. Parmesan, grated

1 head Romaine lettuce, thinly sliced
½ pint cherry tomatoes, quartered
1 English cucumber, diced
2 boneless/skinless chicken breasts
6 – 12 inch spinach tortillas

Directions:

1. Bring 4 cups water to a boil. Add chicken breasts and reduce heat. Simmer for 25-30 minutes.

2. Shred and cut chicken into bite-sized pieces.

3. Meanwhile combine first 6 ingredients above for your Caesar dressing. Toss dressing with thinly sliced Romaine lettuce.

4. Combine salad, tomatoes, and chicken. Season with salt and pepper.

5. Roll in a spinach tortilla.

Cooking.
Magical.
Fun.

Create your own summer recipe.

Ingredients

Prep time:___minutes   **Total time:**___minutes

Yields ____ servings

"Celebrate cooking with seasonal fruits and vegetables." ~ *Mrs. Sheff*

Chicken Lettuce Wraps

Summertime lettuce wraps are a perfect summer meal. They are fast and delicious to whip up during the week.

Prep time: 10 minutes   **Total time:** 30 minutes

Yields 10-12 servings

2 Tbsp. canola oil
1 clove garlic, *minced*
1 lb. ground chicken
2 Tbsp. hoisin sauce
4 Tbsp. low sodium soy sauce

1 tsp. sesame oil
1 carrot, *finely shredded*
Red cabbage, *finely shredded*
1 bunch scallions, *cut diagonally*
1 head crispy iceberg lettuce

Directions:

1. Sauté garlic, scallions and chicken in canola oil over medium heat.

2. Add in hoisin sauce, soy sauce and sesame oil.

3. Top with shredded carrots and red cabbage.

4. Serve in a crispy iceberg lettuce leaf.

About the Author

Cindy Sardo is a teacher at heart especially when it comes to teaching children to cook and eat healthy. Her inspirations to write these children's cook books are many, but her finicky eater, Sarah, has been the greatest. Before becoming a mom, she was a fourth grade classroom teacher for ten years. These experiences made for an excellent recipe to begin writing the Cooking's Cool collection. When she is not writing recipes or cooking creative meals for her family, she can be found around town with three little ladies—Emily, Julia and Sarah. She lives in Landenberg, Pennsylvania with her husband Dave and their beagle Jack.

To learn more about Cooking's Cool visit us at

cookingscool.com

t f 📷

COOKING'S COOL

Feeding Kids Well

68532277R00060

Made in the USA
Middletown, DE
21 September 2019